T0018480

ᑌᑎᏏᎧ

OSKANA POETRY & POETICS

Aaron Kreuter

Shifting Baseline
Syndrome

University of Regina Press

Cover art: Cyber fish designed by Andy Verboom. Retro television public domain.

Cover and text design: Duncan Campbell, University of Regina Press

Editor: Randy Lundy
Proofreader: Donna Grant

The text and titling faces are Arno, designed by Robert Slimbach.

creative
SASKATCHEWAN

Library and Archives Canada Cataloguing in Publication

Title: Shifting baseline syndrome / Aaron Kreuter.

Names: Kreuter, Aaron, author.

Series: Oskana poetry & poetics ; 13.

Description: Series statement: Oskana poetry & poetics ; 13

Identifiers: Canadiana (print) 20210369205 | Canadiana (ebook) 20210369213 | ISBN 9780889778542 (softcover) | ISBN 9780889778559 (PDF) | ISBN 9780889778566 (EPUB)

Subjects: LCGFT: Poetry.

Classification: LCC PS8621.R485 S55 2022 | DDC C811/.6—dc23

UNIVERSITY OF REGINA PRESS
University of Regina
Regina, Saskatchewan
Canada S4S 0A2
TELEPHONE: (306) 585-4758
FAX: (306) 585-4699
WEB: www.uofrpress.ca
EMAIL: uofrpress@uregina.ca

We acknowledge the support of the Canada Council for the Arts for our publishing program. We acknowledge the financial support of the Government of Canada. / Nous reconnaissons l'appui financier du gouvernement du Canada. This publication was made possible with support from Creative Saskatchewan's Book Publishing Production Grant Program.

For Noa

Some days I can feel the sheer unwatchable amount of television expanding all around me, it's like humidity.

—Emily Nussbaum, Twitter

There is a name, coined by the fisheries scientist Daniel Pauly, for this forgetting: "Shifting Baseline Syndrome."

—George Monbiot, *Feral: Rewilding the Land, the Sea and Human Life*

Fluidity of memory and a capacity to forget is perhaps the most haunting trait of our species.

—Wade Davis, "The Unraveling of America"

I. Like Humidity

II. Just Another Name for Anthropocene

III. The Last River

I

LIKE HUMIDITY

We were young and we were reckless and we wanted to see the ice
before it melted.

When the power went out we had nowhere to plug in our vaporizer,
so we reverted back to apples, magnifying glasses, conversation.

Sam's new, dry lips scratched my face and I came, right in my green
cords, but wait: I guess I should start at the beginning.

After the fall, we spent our days breaking dams, daylighting rivers,
freeing chickens, nights warm at the fire, secretly missing television.

It was perverse, what can we say, there is no excuse: we wanted the
collapse to happen in our lifetime. The first of many terrible guilts.

I am not ready. I am not ready. I am not ready. I am not ready. I am not
ready. I am not ready. I am not ready. I am not ready yet.

That was the summer we were most alive. Now, marbled with cancer,
we wait for the only thing that ever scared us. Relief.

We first met at the airport; you were arriving, I was departing. Well no, that's not true. We met at the docks. You had a snow globe of the shtetl on your back, I had a journal of poetry written in Yiddish, Judeo-Arabic, Ladino, Biblical and military Hebrew, all in my worst Rashi script. Okay, that's not exactly how it happened. We met at a family reunion, did the math, discovered we were eighteenth cousins fourth or fifth removed— eh, we threw exactness to the wind, joked that at least we weren't seventeenth cousins, fell in love over Montreal cheese bagels and obscure rock 'n' roll. Fine. You got me. That's a lie. The truth: we met in the MEC parking lot. We met outside the walls of Jericho, ready to defect. We met outside the cave, you sapien I neanderthal, your brother had just killed my parents, we ate spaghetti and made up stories about the stars. We met behind the shopping mall's loading dock, our forest selves sick with horror. We met at the dawn of the Upper Silurian, you were a fresh-jawed fish, I was a giant scorpion, all elbows. We met on the shore, you still tasted of salt, slick and briny, were still wobbly on new legs, I was the biggest tree you've ever seen, had come out of the bath a few eons early to get dinner ready. We met at a deep sea vent some four billion summers ago, first cousins at last, finally ready to subdivide. From there, things got difficult, if you know what I mean (some arms of the family just have a better sense of life's dining-room table). The farther out along the endless river delta we go, the less likely our encounter—yet everywhere we look, the spark from that first meeting, the mitochondria slipping into the soft-walled eukaryote, the smashing of glass, the groaning of the mantel, the asteroid and the oven, the pipeline and the smokestack, the iceberg and the volcano, a handmade guitar named the Sixth Extinction, the web in the high corner above our bed as we tell—for the trillionth and final time—the story of our love.

A cup of coffee was always a dollar fifty. The fisheries were always stocked with the same amount of fish as when I was a little kid with a little kid's obsession with the ocean. From the windows of an airplane the Great Lakes were always noosed in four-lane highways. The land was always distributed in neat, tight little stamps. There were never any birds here. A moose was always a rare sighting. The bats were always dying. The wilderness was always accessible for the day rate of twelve fifty a car, and the highly reasonable seasonal rate of a hundred and fifteen. Speaking of cars, there were always cars. There were always tailing ponds. There were always spiderwebs of six-lane highways, eight-lane highways, ten-lane highways. There were always continents. There were always oil spills visible from space. There were always clearcuts the exact shape and size of Kansas. We were always one heartbeat away from cancer. There was always somebody to hate and always a reasonable way to hate them. Our baselines haven't shifted—you have. We were always hemmed in by landfill, our rivers were always flammable, our lakes always figments of our imagination. There was always a view from the airplane window. Always.

We avoid spoilers like we avoid Lake Ontario,
best-before dates, the evening news.
Spoilers are the hottest blaspheme of the day;
spoilers are us at our best worst selves.
Don't spoil this for me, the twenty-first century
says to the twenty-fourth, I'm still three
seasons behind. (As if it isn't obvious
that the alien planet ends up being
a simulation, that the president is a robot,
that our favourite breakfast smoothie
is poisoning the planet one guava at a time.)
Is it really the future we are afraid of spoiling—
who betrays whom and who kills what and who fucks where?—
or is it something else,
something going rotten in the back
of the universe's refrigerator?
Just as correspondence chess games,
each move predicated on the lunch breaks
of mail carriers, becomes a game
played online with someone in Dubai
over a three-minute blackberry danish,
narrative time collapses into the spondee of
play all, the sugary crunch of *binge*
(this *means* something, you write
in your viewing journal—but *what?*).
We look away, we watch three hundred episodes
of *Who Wants to Be a Parking Lot Attendant?*,
we distract ourselves from the difficult
writers-room slog that's surely ahead of us:
to craft a series' ending that is thematically
consistent, that is narratively fresh, that is just.
That closes our solipsistic dreamtime
with the sweetest possible decomposition.

These times we live in, I'm telling you, it's not right. Just look at the internet. A young boy's first experience with a river used to be something special, something formative, something sweet and innocent. That first glimpse of curling blue through the trees. Getting down to the rocky shore, seeing the current for the first time. Throwing in a pebble, wading in, full of wanting to know what happens around the bend. The moment fresh water bursts into estuary. And now? Now within a minute of opening up a browser they can surf an infinite number of rivers, in all stages of flow! From an underground stream to a roaring headwater, these kids' minds are being perverted by the sheer infinitude of our waterways. How can we expect our young ones to have a healthy relationship to their river once they have been shown the unlimited possibilities that are just a click away! Not to mention, of course, the exploited rivers themselves. I'm telling you, these times we live in.

A DAY IN THE LIFE OF A
HIGH COMPLEXITY BURN BOSS

*A High Complexity Burn Boss with extensive experience with
prescribed burning will conduct the burn with a qualified crew.*

—A "Prescribed Burn Notice" from the City of Toronto

From a young age fire was my friend,
and now I take its toss and swirl
and wield it like a hose. The forest floor
burns like a carpet of gold, like a
sea of effervescent foam, like
the burnt skin of our abandoned god,
and I? I hold the key, the switch,
the sacred knowledge of pyrotechnics
I bestow with firm mercy.
If conditions are favourable, the smoke
will stream upwards in a tight cylinder,
a portal of ash straight to the manna-laced heavens.
If the conditions are not favourable,
the city will taste like barbecue
for weeks. Either way, we get paid.
My high complexity burn crew has read
all the holy books, all the technical minutiae. Yes,
we are a tight, focused unit. Yes,
my leadership is unquestioned. Yes,
our mantra is simple: Destroy in order
to create. Unleash death to feed life. Wield fire
to contain, to manicure, to bless our desired flora,
eviscerate what we have deemed waste.
At night, my suit airing out in the backyard,

I watch commercials for yogurt
and pharmaceuticals, fall asleep television-bared,
dream of golf courses that I shape
with a flick of the hand, the green,
green grass catching the sun
like the very cup that brimmeth over.

I will not mention the midnight sun. There will be no geysers amid steaming earth-wounds, no allusions to the Sagas, no glaciers melting into rivers dropping into waterfalls pooling into coastal plains snuggling into our hearts. There will be no black sand. (As is standard in the genre, there will be no Icelanders either.) So we luxuriated in porta-potty-hued waters? So we bathed in a piss-hot river in a steady downpour, halfway between sleep and bliss? So we took to the farm-abutted roads with touristy malice? So we fucked on a volcano—so what? No one said this sweater was going to be easy. What we're left with: a yellow road sign with a city silhouette crossed out in definitive red. A giftshop GIF of a volcanic island denuded of ninety-nine percent of its trees bursting with invasive purple carpets of Arctic lupine. Sulphur burbs and scorched savings accounts. Neon yellow bananas bred in Colombia, bought in a grocery store in Grindavík, ripened on guesthouse windowsills but never eaten, flown back to Toronto in a plane named after the volcano that one eon or another will smother us out of existence, baked into muffins laced with chocolate chips and walnuts, eaten by a lake two hours north of the city, that, despite everything, most certainly remembers.

THIS MEETING OF THE WESTEROS
ENVIRONMENTAL ALLIANCE IS CALLED TO ORDER

There's something about those Wildlings
that's just so, ya know, wild.
All that open space, all
that proximity to non-human life,
it just makes you want to dance.
What would people south of the wall
know of that, eh, John Snow?

King's Landing has just slashed
funding for the Dorne Nature Reserve.
Now we'll have to go someplace else
for our hit of untouched super-pristine eco-splendour,
our weekly cure for our hereditary nature-deficit disorder.

Winter is coming, says
the climate change denier
to the executioner with a soft spot
for paddling gentle-hearted rivers.
Winter is coming, says the biologist
with the latest statistics on specicide.
Winter is coming, says the door-to-
door furnace saleswoman.

(Anybody who's anybody knows
that the drowned god drives a Tesla.)

I swear to you,
by the old gods and the new,
that pissing against a white pine
after a night spent by a fire
after a hard day's hike
is one of the finest pleasures in this
doomed and dooming world.

One could argue that every essential modern conception
is based on a conception of "meanwhile."

—Benedict Andersen, Imagined Communities

Meanwhile, Carmella gets a crash-course in quantum computing.
Meanwhile, Homer and Marge argue about the nuclear codes they
    accidentally won in the town raffle.
Meanwhile, Dawson heads deep into Trump Country incognito to report
    for his blog, Dawson's Dispatches (unique monthly visitors: 15).
Meanwhile, Victor and Nick prepare for their inaugural journey to the
    International Space Station.
Meanwhile, Mac and Dennis's collaborative dissertation is *not* going well.
Meanwhile, Sally Draper-Francis, a month after her discharge from
    Sea Shepherd, walks into the desert east of LA with nothing in her
    backpack but two dozen bananas, ten grapefruits, a sheet of acid,
    and a notebook.
Meanwhile, Lindsay leaves for her first Grateful Dead concert, but,
    thanks to the TV gods, will never get there, will forever be alert and
    expectant in that blue minivan, Zeno at the wheel.
Meanwhile, the mice living in the back of the oven decide to finally start
    writing down their history.
Meanwhile, the balsam fir colonizes another warming valley.
Meanwhile, two feet of water is enough to make us seriously question
    the quaintness of rural gas stations.
Meanwhile, a hundred billion galaxies of a hundred billion stars pull a
    little farther apart from each other.
Meanwhile, the universe expands and collapses endlessly until in some
    deep-sea vent or shallow pool Life is born, and with it Time.
Meanwhile, we wonder (as always)
if anything else
            is on.

BONETOWN

Like all accidental apocalypses,
it started as a joke. Bonetown?
I'd ask. Bonetown! you'd respond.
(Our eyes on the screen.)

How were we to know, all those years
ago, that bonetown was more than just
a glance between two characters
who would soon be getting it on,

that bonetown was a terminal destination,
the painful result of our human experiment
in exponential growth, our delirious fucking
ourselves right into the rag-and-bone-town

of the grave? We couldn't. Or, rather,
we wouldn't. We were too busy waiting for
the next surprise coupling, the next
sexy instance of television-logic desire,

the weather announcer smiling
during the commercial break as they repeated
the long-term forecast: low down,
blown crown, bonetown.

Plastic spaceship, time-capsule phone booth. Last townhouse in a row bordering a suburb of tents, a downtown of hill and stage. Blue walls, sweet cloying disinfectant. The escalator inside you is a thermal vent is a lake heated to boil is an eye gone full pupil. Something shifts outside, changing the light, and you're a lone outpost on the moon. You're a coat-check girl in her little cubby deep in Marianas Trench. You're trapped under two kilometres of glacial ice (the ice is heavy, calm, aquamarine). There's a knock on the door—it's the ice wanting to get in, wanting to scratch you, mark you, gargle boulder potholes into your skin. (From far away, laughter.) Something shifts. Time forgets itself. Your vertical tub fills with fossils, skeletons, detritus of a trillion spines, a trillion spins, the sweet heady reek of endlessly proliferating biomass, clacking and jostling—a knock on the door. Time slows to the wind-smoothed peak of a single heartbeat. Remember your breath, remember your feet on the ground, your skirt bunched at your knees, your hair in its tight summertime bun, the music that waits outside the grey door you will touch as little as possible; remember to wipe. Release yourself to joy. Outside, something shifts. The world glows blue. You leak everything from everywhere.

SURE-FIRE SIGNS YOUR LOVED ONE IS A SMARTPHONE USER

When you ask why her pants are vibrating
she says she ate too many beans last night,
then leaves the room, her hand on her pocket.

You wake up in the middle of the night
to find him under the covers, which are glowing.
In the morning his thumbs are chapped.

Commercials about the dangers of second-hand
smartphone use send your loved one to the kitchen,
where she loudly puts away the dishes:

ten minutes later he says he's going
for a walk; hours pass, and when he climbs into bed
he stinks of radiation and Listerine.

You discover smartphone chargers plugged
into sockets in the furnace room,
the attic, hidden in the garage behind the firewood.

The tension soars. You air out the cars,
have midnight panic attacks for the children's health.
The landline rings and you fear confrontation.

CAPITALISM GETS AN ORIGIN STORY

After Patricia Lockwood

Here's the pitch. Before big, bad capitalism is what we know it as today, who was capitalism? What were capitalism's lazy summer days at the fair like? What *happened* to capitalism? Interesting. I'm listening. So, what, does capitalism have some kind of lovable, eccentric family? Oh yeah. Big time. Rebellious sister, unfulfilled mother, racist father. Alright. Okay. Let's hear some episode arcs. Capitalism is involved in a merry mix-up. Capitalism witnesses a rape at its high school: what does capitalism do? Capitalism spreads across the globe, turning everything solid into thin air. Capitalism's parents throw capitalism a surprise party, but capitalism had a bad day at school (failed an economics exam) and throws a tantrum, capitalism's father grills cheeseburgers dejectedly, the sun setting behind him as the credits roll. How about a whole golden-age-of-television angle? Capitalism as the masculine monster? Soft-spoken, a family man, a violent psychopath with a hundred dead bodies buried beside the swimming pool? Great, great, just great. The bigwigs are going to love this. We're going to be buried in ratings reviews revenue renown! We're going to do for capitalism what capitalism did to the Middle Passage. We're going to out-capital capital. Because you can't spell capitalism without someone, somewhere, getting fucked.

How easy to forget that we're here because of maps, that map libraries are dangerous places. Maps can lead you directly to the clear-cut or they can show you how to run the river without leaving a trace. Maps tell us denizens of the twenty-first a too-familiar story: from reckless diversity to white-orange-and-grey soft monolith (seventeen clicks from the street corner where you almost had your first kiss to the flat false television screen of the globe). A satellite image of the Great Lakes is to the Great Lakes as the phrase "eight billion people" is to eight billion *actual* people, if you want to get homologous about it. Maps don't colonize people, assholes colonize people (with the help of maps, of course). Maps are a story we tell ourselves in our most mapless moments. The portage around the rapids is off by two millimetres and therefore you will die. There's a smudge on the screen where there's supposed to be a weapons factory and, whoopsie, there goes a children's hospital. A map's relation to mystery depends entirely on the mapmaker's commitment to a solid breakfast. Maps lie. Or they don't.

II

JUST ANOTHER NAME
FOR ANTHROPOCENE

Dearest Muffy: As I hinted in my last letter to you and your brother, the discovery I felt we were on the very brink of making has indeed been made! All the years spent studying, arguing, all those on my team who gave their time and left their families for a hunch, a vision—it has all paid off! (If only your darling mother were still with us to eat the fruit of our labour.) Muffy, it's more momentous than we could ever have hoped: in the third antechamber off the main room—you remember, don't you, you yourself posited that this room could be of some importance—we have found a library of sorts. Not books like our libraries, now, but sheaves of rough parchment, organized on shelves. But, ho ho—this is nothing as compared to what is *on* these textiles! For, as alluded to in various ancient documents, the people—or peoples—who left us this find had a written language, but it is like nothing I—or I dare say, anybody—has ever encountered. The language is fully composed of what appears to be rivers. Going from left to right, then curving right to left, so on and so forth, page after page of rivers, never repeating, never without another surprise as it snakes down the page. To my untrained eye, I can identify rapids of varying intensity, forks and reconvergences, narrows, widths, islands big and small, rock gardens, at least forty-five variety of tree (I wonder, is it possible that the current native inhabitants are *descended* from these river gods? Seems unlikely, though I must say, they know the rivers in these parts better than any Brit I've ever met!). My dear Muffy, do you realize what this means? My tenure at Cambridge is all but guaranteed. Ha ha! Thousands and thousands of pages. What does it mean? What does it all *mean*? It could take us another three generations to decipher the linguistic syntax (and who knows what the political situation will be like by then, the way they're talking at Parliament). Nothing like it has been discovered in the last fifty years! It is times like these that I miss your dear mother more than anything. How can I not help but think of those spring afternoon picnics by the river near the fen, during our early courtship? Listen to me, boring you with the reminiscences of an old man. Ah well. Let our human knowledge progress, at all costs. Send regards to your brother. Love, Charles Kingchair.

The professor of ontology doesn't hold formal office hours. The professor of ontology doesn't make appointments; he's either available to meet, or he isn't. The professor of ontology is colour-blind. The professor of ontology sees things through the lens of being and not-; there is no other legitimate criteria. The professor of ontology has a weekly political column. The professor of ontology has dabbled a little in history, a little in economics. The professor of ontology doesn't understand why these people hate us so. The professor of ontology will redraw the map of the city to keep its citizens safe (the subsequent walls and security checkpoints and people's army are not the professor of ontology's department). The professor of ontology says that we are a small nation of superheroes surrounded by an endless sea of supervillains. The professor of ontology says that, yes, in ontology such distinctions are possible. The professor of ontology sadly admits that, sometimes, violence is the only way to make these people understand. The professor of ontology says that the field of ontology is okay with this. The professor of ontology knows that withholding abortions, offering child incentives, defunding schools, yes, even forced sterilization in a pinch, is okay in order to keep a democratic majority. The professor of ontology once had a torrid love affair with a graduate student named Dan at an archaeological site in enemy territory (this was in the professor of ontology's younger, wilder days). The professor of ontology's wife—sometimes referred to as the first lady of ontology—does not know, though she suspects. The professor of ontology recommends four square inches of freshly killed meat every night. The professor of ontology has a pet parakeet. The professor of ontology is a very busy man. The professor of ontology has been dabbling in orthodontics. The professor of ontology will see you now.

Language is a virus from outer space. It landed on Earth sometime after its cousin the asteroid thought it would be fun to kill off the dinosaurs, but sometime before James Joyce drafted *Ulysses*. Language is a virus from outer space. It's passed on from parent to child, generation to generation, pirate to parrot and back again. Language is a virus from outer space. It colonized us so completely that we don't even realize with each new utterance we are feeding it, making it stronger. The more words for "take-out" there are, the happier the language virus. Thankfully, there is a cure. To bring down a tower, you block all exits but one and lay siege. And since that time when the sun never set, we are closer than ever to that single door. Once English is the only language left, think how easy it will be to contain, inoculate, eradicate. Then we will be free to spread out into the cosmos, bringing our hard-earned transcendent wisdom to every corner of the universe. Because language is a virus, and it taught us all we know.

THE LAST SIX MINUTES OF THE
NATURE DOCUMENTARY, WHERE DAVID
ATTENBOROUGH TELLS US THE BEAUTIFUL
ANIMALS WE'VE JUST BEEN WATCHING ARE
GOING EXTINCT, AND IT'S ALL OUR FAULT

It takes thousands of hours,
untold boxes of Clif Bars,
an undisclosed number of wet dreams
in a pup tent on the soft furry side of a mountain
to get that one perfect shot.
But get them we do.
And for what, so you can
ooh and aah
while eating BBQ chicken
and then fall asleep
until your television
asks "Are You Still Watching?"
Well, it is a good question.
Are you asleep?
Are you still watching?
You do know that the animals
on your infants' onesies
and crib sheets are going the way
of the telegram, don't you?
You understand
that once the ice is gone
say goodbye to
perfectly chilled negronis,
to a little soothing comfort during labour,
to coastal cities and island nations?
You fools,
you cephalopods,
nature isn't dying,
it's simply revising

its target audience.
And in the new series,
there will be no winnowing
down from all that expectant waiting
to that one hyper-edited
moment of animal glory,
no swelling horns
or contemplative strings,
no old British sophisticated me:
it'll be long,
it'll be messy,
it'll be incoherent and deeply, truly unfair,
the ocean (like in all the best episodes)
will be involved,
and, perhaps worst of all,
there will be nowhere left
for you to send the hate mail.

It's all TV now, or so the TV pundits say. What they won't say: that not all alternate histories are the same degree of alternate. That the showrunners let the books dictate the episodes until there's no more books and then all they're left with is their penises to guide them. That a television show has never ended properly because television shows never end. On the weather channel a skywriter writes in looping cuneiform a message from the higher realms: "It was one of the great TV genres, until it wasn't." The fine print: television is no longer merely a physical object, a screen and a power adapter and cathode ray tubes. Television is a metaphysics. Television is the fine arm hairs of the zeitgeist you can only see in certain afternoon light. Television is just another name for Anthropocene. You get home and turn on the news, 'cause why not ruin a perfectly shitty day? On one channel they yell that left-handed people are not human. On the other channel they debate if mountains look better with the mountaintops removed. Sometimes the death and hypocrisy seem almost real. Sometimes the talking heads bare their souls, sometimes the desertification is nearly complete, sometimes you ask yourself: what *is* an automobile? And always, always, always, the chyron looping along the bottom one-fifteenth of your screen with those five magic words. *Television, get away from me.*

I.

You get it, right?
Auschwitz is a *symbol*.
It's that symbol he destroys.
No, it doesn't matter what
it's a symbol *for*—
I can't believe you'd even ask me that—
because in the context
of the movie it just makes
perfect narrative *sense*.
Do you get it? Auschwitz is a
symbol. It's that symbol
he destroys. A symbol
for, for . . . for something or other. How
many times do I have to
explain it?

II.

For this shoot we need balance. Balance, balance, balance. And insane carnage swaddled in massive symphonic music. Now Michael, who are you? Yes, you're Magneto. But you're also Eric. Eric, Magneto, Michael. In that order. And Ian. Can't forget old Ian. Your young Polish family was just killed by incompetent policemen in a freak accident in the woods, let's not forget this. Use it. You were tortured here, your mother was killed in front of you, here. Remember? Remember? Use it. You ate a terrible eggplant parmagiana sandwich yesterday? Use it! You're doing this for them, for the dead, the tortured, all those horrifically murdered eggplants—I mean, dead. Horrifically murdered dead. Alrighty? Great. And—roll camera!

III.

The movie? Terrible.
The scene? Horrendous.
The acting? Laughable.
The genocidal shark? Jumped.
My ire? Raised.
The special effects? Spectacular.

IV.

No Nazis were harmed
in the making of this revenge fantasy.

V.

Can you be a misanthrope
if in their eyes
you are not even human?

VI.

The rabbi is dead.
The tribes have recalled their ambassadors.
Your answering machine is full.
Still, I'll go on.

VII.

The dream of revenge.
The reality of mutation.
The nightmare of power.

VIII.

What would my grandfathers (never met) think of this?
What would Herzl think of this?
What would my Palestinian cousin in diaspora think of this?
What would Hoss?
Maimonides?
Rachel?
Someone not wearing these *meshugana*
3D glasses?

IX.

Of course it should be destroyed.
Of course we are complicit.
Of course those buildings should be ripped
from the earth like so many blighted trees,
not to mention that museum.
Of course Auschwitz is an idea
and like any idea once brick-and-mortared
will remain in trace amounts
in the air, in the soil, in the seas,
no matter what mutant's rage.

X.

This is the furnace
in which I was forged.
I will burn it down.

XI.

The folly of furnaces.
The human folly of furnaces.

XII.

A chess game with the professor
might calm you down.
A world that makes sense.
Where nothing is hidden,
nothing lurking,
festering,
waiting.

XIII.

Don't forget Oscar Isaac.
He's there too,
behind those matte car doors.

XIV.

Leaving the villa in Wannsee,
my whole body electric.
How can I resist telling Evie?
Both of us stunningly alive,
alive, alive. Alive in History.

XV.

Leaving the gift shop,
a sickening realization:
you forgot to buy
the Crematorium II keychain
for your nephew.
Oh, what a world!

XVI.

Dreams of steel and tin.
The pull of the moon.
A neutron star humming.
Something unseen,
gathering.

XVII.

Concentration camps. Death centres. Killing fields. Auction blocks. Displaced persons camps. Residential schools. Urban ghettos. Blast zones. Destruction radii. Fallout. No man's land. Museums. Memorials. Plinths. Pit mines. Strip mines. Vertical shaft single stage hoisting mines. Ethnic enclaves. Islands of plastic in seas of nuclear waste. Sound stages. Green screens. Movie theatres. Smart screens. Supermarkets. Checkpoints.

XVIII.

She rustled in her sleep.
She murmured in a language thought dead.
She sighed deeply.
She dreamed on.

Like so many of our great deceased men, Theodor Herzl returned to us on Twitter. At first it was mostly a platform for jokes. "Hey, who moved my body?" "So much for utopia, am I right?!" But then he stumbled upon the FreePalestine hashtag. But then he discovered what PEP stands for. So he unfollowed Ben-Gurion. He unfollowed the real Netanyahu, the parody Netanyahu. He unfollowed the ADL. He tweeted about the possibility of a hashtag so powerful, so full of potential justice, that with one tweet the crisis would simply cease (if you will it, so forth and so on). Herzl overreacts to the bombing of a hospital. Herzl declares his support for BDS. Herzl writes a twitter essay on context collapse. Herzl overreacts to the bombing of a school. Herzl gets reported for hate speech. Herzl gets doxed (leading Herzl to tweet out that he now understands what it's like to be a woman—Oh, Herzl!). Herzl gets called a self-hating Jew supervillain communist neoliberal abortionist Jewy scum terrorist Jew. Herzl gets retweeted by Nazis. Well, Herzl's had enough. Herzl's had it up to here. Herzl's leaving Twitter. Herzl's going to give 4chan a try.

We all know it's there, off-screen,
though most of us haven't seen it, off-screen.
Would we even know what it looks like, off-screen?
Behind-the-scenes is not quite the same thing as off-screen.
Invisible-slash-unseen is not the same ontological position
    as off-screen.
I double-dog dare you to write a political sestina with all
    end-words off-screen.
All the ladies in the club say, *off-screen.*
All the fellas in the club shout, *off-screen.*
Yeah, I see you there, off-screen.
Is there something in my teeth, here, off-screen?
Whole provincial parks of off-screen
lead to visions of lives lived off-screen,
end in panic attacks at the cessation of the possibility of off-screen.
Entire continents clamouring for the exit off-screen.
Whole floors of skyscrapers working for their own financial and
    sexual benefit off-screen.
Toxic waste and coffee cups piling up off-screen.
Off-gassing mostly affects people off-screen, mostly.
The protests are taking place just off-screen.
It's another world, isn't it, off-screen.
What a scream, off-screen.

Waiting for the results of the core samples, we already know the news isn't good. How could it be good? The phone rings and rings, which must mean they're all dead. The power blows, and here we are, catatonic on the pull-out, our go-bag forgotten. Our hearts skip a beat and that's it, get us to the hospital. Hello, my name is Sisyphus, and I'm a perpetual failure. How is it possible that this bad mood will not be the final mood? How will the storm ever end? How will the doctor not say, "The swelling, I'm afraid, is here to stay"? The meth lab in our cortexes is currently in overproduction of a drug called *too much*, but what are we supposed to do, call the fucking cops? Our post-punk band Cognitive Distortions has a show in Denmark, but the airline lost our pedal board, and without distortion what are we but a bunch of trembling, fearful musicians who can't even read music? Our program has three steps. Step one: relax. Step two: talk ourselves down/put things into perspective. Step three: choose an action to affect the outcome of the situation. Unless, of course, you're not overreacting, then forget the whole thing, let Panic, that willful teenager who abstained from jacking-off for a week and now has lost his proverbial marbles, take the pre-verbal wheel. We no longer believe that the planet is what it is through a series of sudden disasters—even though how right does this feel, how true? The forest changes too fast for us to notice, too slow for us to set our watches to. The heat wave is infernal, the cold snap eternal. The forest fire will always be just outside the fire-retardant door. We could try to do something about it, but what's the point. The worst is already here, in all its present perfect glory. *How don't you see it?* we yell to our nieces on the newly reinstalled houseline. The Earth is dying. The Earth is dead. The Earth is, has been, and always will be.

It's as if an earthquake
spat steel, glass,
and designer couches
out of the ground,
pushed the whole package
into a coastal skyline of high-rises
in a mere elevator-door blink of geological time
(only a select few surfing
the ensuing tidal wave of wealth).
Standing in the surf
you feel their monstrosity
as creeping shadows.
Were there ever *not*
traffic lights, underground parking lots,
proscribed squares of "natural growth,"
sprinklers tossing rainbows,
rainbows, rainbows?
At the restaurants,
yachts move like sleek lozenges
down our peripherals.
Sure, there are neighbourhoods
away from the shores and the malls,
sure, there are lives not
predicated on advanced lefts
to the strip mall, to the golf course,
to the seafood restaurant
where crab legs start at fifty dollars,
sure, sure, sure,
but for the week you are here
you exist between the intracoastal
and the sea,

between salt and sand,
between steel and sky.
You close your eyes and pretend
the buildings aren't there,
but it won't take. The buildings *are* there.
A plane planes by, dragging an American flag
big enough to smother the sky.
Still, you can bike
into a cold sugary wind
before stopping for tacos and a swim.
Still, you can take the elevator
to the beach with a book
on the failures of international justice,
swim in the pulling surf,
drink water from an icy thermos.
Still, you can take the elevator
back up to the condo,
sticky and exhausted.
You can take a shower.
You can open a browser.
You can type:
The First Seminole War.
The Second Seminole War.
The Third Seminole War.

MY FATHER PHILOSOPHIZES ABOUT THE OCEAN
TO STEPH'S AUNT AND UNCLE, WHO WE JUST RAN
INTO AT THE CHEESECAKE FACTORY AND WHO,
AFTER TELLING US ABOUT THEIR POST-BREAST-
REDUCTION SEX LIFE USING QUITE GRAPHIC
LANGUAGE, MENTIONED THEY NEVER GO TO THE
BEACH, EVEN THOUGH HERE WE ARE, IN FLORIDA

What you have to understand is, the ocean is immense. The ocean is a living thing. To the ocean, we are nothing, we are dust. There are no walls in the ocean. This is worth repeating. There are no walls in the ocean. You take the elevator down from your rented condo, you walk through the pool area, you open the gate and enter the beach, the sand hot and vital on your feet. You step into the ocean. You take another step. You submerge. You swim out till you are over your head, and you tread water, you float there treading water facing out, facing the vast expanse. You find that part of you that is most closed and, with the ocean's great gentle guidance, you open it, you open it, you open it as you tread water facing out, facing the vast expanse. As fucked up as the world is, as long as there is ocean, it's a world I want to be in. To the ocean, we are nothing, we are dust. There are no walls. In the ocean. What you have to understand. The immensity. The vastness. The immense vastness. Hmm? Yes, you too. Enjoy your cheesecake.

III

THE LAST RIVER

CÔTE SAINT-LUC ROAD

Looking out the window late Friday night,
the ninth-floor apartment a watchtower
on the border between downtown and the suburbs,
wondering about the cars going by:
suburban teenage Jews perhaps, like I once was,
driving home from the city,
the corner of Sainte-Catherine and Saint-Laurent
carpeted with thousands of glinting watch batteries—
or have I fallen through the cracks
of this weird night (three a.m. and unable
to sleep, the city churning below me),
and am watching my mother's car
return from my father's small apartment on University,
chili on the stove, a music stand, clarinet reeds
sprinkled around the room like maple keys
(they fell in love at the symphony, hands
grasped in a tumult of horns, icy sidewalks);
or it's my father himself, taxiing home
from Friday night dinner at my mother's
family duplex (not far from here),
a meal to mark the end of the week;
there goes my uncle,
then eighteen, blasted on '71 pot
and in love again, The Beatles
on the radio, so full of the world
my grandmother's basement
was never going to contain him.

MONTREAL

For Edna Borden, 1923–2016

My grandmother whistles as she pads through the kitchen.
I'm at the island reading the Mordecai Richler stories

I found in the basement, tales of working-class Jews living
in a narrow strip of Montreal knotted around St. Urbain Street,

a crowded hallway between the old world and the Quebecois.
My grandmother knows these stories, she grew up in one,

the pages of her teenage years a two-bedroom walk-up
on Mount Royal, her older sisters asleep on a hideabed

in the living room while she lies open-eyed in the room
she shares with her parents, listening to the Kogans bicker

in Yiddish from the extra room they rent out, I once
walked those streets on my way home from a poetry reading,

a lull during a winter rainstorm, the snow and rain frozen over,
from every branch, bush, and staircase ice hung like sharp tears,

the street crystallized and alien, the ground a frictionless mirror.
My grandmother puts away the dishes as her parents disembark

early from their Chicago-bound boat, my great-aunt sick
with the measles, and Quebec City inherits five new bodies;

I close the book and watch the water as the steamer leaves
the St. Lawrence, climbs over the Atlantic, docks in the port city

pointed towards the inland roads, I sniff for the shtetl
in the hard edges of the kitchen. There's my grandmother's

Yiddish, the cinnamon buns baked yearly to break the fast,
the particular build of my face, my cousins' faces, and what else—

the sun from the picture window sweeps in, brooms the dust
into the corners, the book waits in my lap, heavy like a ship's log,

my grandmother finally sits down, from my perch in the kitchen
I can see to the front door, the quiet streets, the grooved world.

Six beavers dead,
he says (you floating there),
trapped out. Memories
of last summer:
the day they arrived,
the young at play,
the old at work;
you float there,
playing along.
Now a hundred-pound male
has moved into
the vacant lodge
(the lodge a mere hill
from the dock,
where brambly shore
meets lake,
where you and the dog
once stood on floors
of ice contemplating
hidden winter lives),
is insatiable, unstoppable.
Is toppling every last tree.
He must be trapped out
or rifle-shot or
the property will suffer.
You nod. You float.
You float away.
You go inside,
dream of terrible war,
outlandish death,

righteous human discord,
six beavers swimming
across a still lake
to a new home,
warm,
dry,
safe.

BLACK WALNUT

That first autumn
you rained walnuts
on our roof for weeks.
We'd lie in bed,
scandalously awake,
listening.
Now—how
many years later?—
I watch from the
bathroom window
as men in neon jackets
and harnesses
breach the neighbour's yard,
climb your trunk,
make incision lines,
dismantle you
limb by limb
with whirring saws,
ropes, and house-
shuddering crashes.
After that first season
there were no more walnuts;
we missed the barrage,
the squirrels in their
poses tearing through
the impenetrable bark
with their fast teeth,
the hard evidence
that the world
can indeed take care of itself.
We turned to books,
thought perhaps you were on
a two-year cycle,

a three-year cycle, but then,
last spring, there were
no leaves, the rest of the city
witness to green life.
This year, someone,
somewhere, declared
you dead. Declared you
dangerous. So now
they remove you
into memory.
Your branches
imprinted against
rain-lashed sky.
The dog squaring
off with a family
of overhead raccoons.
Your wide trunk
out the bathroom
window as we shower.
That one year of abundance
we shared. Seeing
you from blocks away,
signifying home.
And now, now a day
of gas-powered motors,
your final falling.
(They won't return
to remove the sawed
sections of trunk for
eight days, feed them
to one of the city's
networked mouths.)
I return to the window

to watch the procession,
return, return again.
Once the work is done,
will I climb the fence,
stand on your engraved stump,
stoop down, count rings?
Probably not. Instead,
I will content myself
with knowing your presence
as loss against the
seasoned sky, imagine
you in a place where the
soil is good, the
rainwater plentiful.
Where the creatures that
live off your plenty are kind,
self-aware,
thankful.

You don't know me
and I don't know you,
but, chances are, we're both twenty-nine,
both still waiting for Marita to find us.
Chances are you, like me,
live in New York, Chicago,
Montreal, Toronto—somewhere on
Turtle Island. Chances are we both
eschew meat, are both fans of dawns
though we don't stay up
late enough or get
up early enough to see them.
(There is also a chance
that none of these chances are true.)
Well, here we are, on either end
of a large divide,
yet still I call out,
still, I say: Hello,
I'm listening. I say: fuck that
soldier at the checkpoint,
fuck that man with a map
and a pen of red ink.
I say: I will do all
that I can—aren't we, after all,
cousins? Maybe when we're 39,
49, 59, 69, once again on the cusp
of some round number,
maybe something will change, shift, (or,
worse) collapse, disintegrate.
Maybe one day we will
hike the land together,
on trails restored and renamed.

We will hike hard morning and afternoon,
drink from streams and wadis,
listen with openness to the
stories of everyone we encounter,
spend the nights by a small fire in the mountains,
the coastal plains, the hills, the desert,
trying to stay up for the sun,
talking, talking, talking.

Parceled out into hour-long dollops,
strung through the weeks, months, years,
and decades, it's not unbearable:

taken all together, a universe de-expanded
into its heavy little fingernail, what becomes

apparent is the scope, the unbelievable web
of baby-snatchings, romances, deaths, intrigues,
family rivalries, repeat romances, fresh blood

from the countryside, network cross-overs—
a barrage of murders, phone calls, living rooms,

cliffhangers, and ominous music. Swallowed in this way,
the essence is revealed: that each marriage,
each divorce, every single betrayal and resurrection,

is nothing but the outcome of narrative pushed
to its edges, plot brought to its logical lunacy:

that without start or end,
on a long enough timeline,
this would be the world.

ALL WE CARE ABOUT IS THE SERIES FINALE
BUT SERIES FINALES ARE ALWAYS TERRIBLE
SO WHY DO WE CONTINUE TO CARE YOU
KNOW WHY IT IS BECAUSE WE ALL SO BADLY
WANT SOMETHING TO BELIEVE IN

We're all television experts now. We know the expected beats like we used to know the seasons. We live for that rare sweet spot, far enough into the show's run that one of the principals has to try to get out of jury duty, not so far that an exotic animal has become a pet. We skip ahead, knowing that all the important stuff happens in the season's final episode, anyways. (Does writing a television show during the end of the world change the rules? we ask our therapists; they respond by saying they don't watch much TV, the worst sentence utterable in nearly any language.) Car doors open; car doors close. Meals are eaten; news is delivered. Think pieces are thought; fan theories are theorized. We salivate for all of it, every coupling, every insensitive joke, every death that hits us harder than the current species die-off. And in between binges and casual viewings and rewatches and random episodes here and there, we dream about what we all want yet what we all fear the most: prime-time cartoons where the characters grow older every season, yet never die.

A glass of water, half full or half empty. Your childhood bathtub, full of poison. A street of milk-chocolate brown puddles after an overnight rainfall nobody saw or heard, a minefield. A sunshower. A rainstorm. A torrential downpour. Tidal waves that heard what you said about them. All the murdered lakes back for horror-movie-style revenge. (Every toilet bowl you pass spooks you into recoil, a porcelain mouth of deranged fangs.) The lake and river systems you once spent happy summers paddling now magma burning with the shrieks of your loved ones. The thirst of a billion throats, heaving oceans of salty fear. Comets of ice slam into the atmosphere, firework into liquid death. You dream nightmares of each one of your hundred trillion cells, swampy nightclubs where every dancing body is a pedophile a murderer a childhood enemy who knows your sexual secrets, you wake up to discover the ice caps have melted your bed afloat on a sea of knives you scream and scream your thirst a stovetop burner levered full blast *water knows no boundaries* you scream *water has skin as soft as pudding as hard as toothache water has sense memory* you holler *from the first spark of 'huh, this is nice' to the last bureaucrat dumping the last load of poison into the last river—from salty womb to wet loam— water's been with us* you stop the roar of rising tides drowning you out the planet drowning you wish for two things one to swing a little farther from the sun all the water sucked up into glorious skyscrapers of ice two to swing just a little closer close enough for it all to evaporate into steam to puff into space leaving everything dry, flopping, crusted. The water sloshes, slaps, spits, and you're finally parched enough to gulp liquid rock.

Our bodies are being mutilated. Our bloodstreams dammed, our lungs drained, our hearts buried in honour of the gods of urban exigency. Our flow pinched, our routes so diverted that the natural unfolding of a life has become a cramped picture postcard of one. Our mental drainage systems so badly disregarded, deflowered, contorted, that organic matter, with nowhere else to go, clogs up, stops up, turns to the blue and white defense of cancer—we are treating our bodies like they belong to us, but what of the upstreaming salmon, the circumspect deer, the vilified beaver, the life forms that we cannot see but are most definitely here? I ask you, once we are dried up completely, what rough monsters will our pebbles, stones, and boulders become without the constant polish of our no-longer-dynamic selves?

Let's fire up our favourite streaming service and watch the newest reality show, ya know, the one about war criminals who make late-in-life career moves. The charismatic general who takes up dog-walking. The founder of Monsanto who starts leading wilderness river trips, cries at every splendiferous sunset. The infamous butcher who runs a vegan fast foodery called Dehumanize This! The show, naturally, is a runaway hit. Because, to get down to brass tacks (which happens to be one of the butcher's preferred methods of torture), aren't war criminals the closest we have to communal myth? Isn't everywhere you look, crime? And so we love war criminals like we love our accountants. True, yes, war criminals do horrible things, they go to war against other war criminals, they commit war crimes—because otherwise what are they doing with such a potent *nom de guerre?*—but they speak our language, they eat our food. They're *our* war criminals. They kiss babies, they plant trees, they have deep, intelligent voices. Our best radio hosts interview the war criminals, say things like "and through all that, you still managed to neutralize your targets?" On evening news shows and Twitter feeds up-and-coming war criminals gregariously pardon older, sort-of-disgraced-but-not-nearly-disgraced-enough war criminals. (With all this focus on war criminals it's easy to miss your neighbour's crimes, your daughter's, your arborist's, yours.) You turn off the television. You turn off your phone. You move to turn off the radio, but then, to your surprise, the radio host introduces a granddaughter of the dispossessed, who responds at length to the claims of the war criminal, her words a flower in the bombed-out rubble blooming into a river into a library into a courthouse into a city you thought could exist only in a dream.

The House Dream

I dream my grandmother as a house. First, she is the various apartments of her childhood: the boarding-houses and tiny one-bedrooms in the Bronx, Coney Island, Brighton Beach. Then, she is the flat in the Red Hook housing projects she and Morty live in as newlyweds (she is nineteen), then the Sheepshead Nostrand Houses they spend fifteen years in, and (finally) I dream that my grandmother is the final destination of her and Morty's climb into the middle class: 53-44 Bell Boulevard, Bayside, Queens. On the map the house is boxed in by highways, service roads, ocean. It is a house full of boys, then a house full of men; a house of argument, of protest, of political hope and political despair; a house of grief; a house of grandchildren visiting from Philadelphia, from Toronto. An attic. A basement.

The City Dream

I'm a child with the eyes and fears of an adult, and she is a dark-skinned woman with the heart of a careening bird, the kind that stays airborne for months at a time. The two of us emerge from the deep darkness of the subway into bright Manhattan. The buildings are dream-large, they are impossibly large. We sit on a bench in a small green park, the city an intricate machine all around us that, thanks to the dreamtime, we instinctively know—skyscrapers so tall and yet still this brightness— and she tells me stories of being a secular Jewish radical in the second half of the twentieth century.

The Mirror Dream

Help! Morty's been dead for thirty years! Thirty years! And Paul, poor Paul, my first child, gone at forty-one. *Help!* We grew up on the beach, ate eggs we fried in the sand—*Help!* she calls, and we don't know whether to laugh or avert our eyes.

The Story Dream

Have I ever told you how we met? she says. A mutual friend introduced us at a Young Communists meeting. Have I ever told you how we met? He was doing work on my house, and we struck up a friendship. Then that incident happened with that lady and they threw him in prison for fifteen years. Oh, did that judge have it out for Puerto Ricans! I visited him, oh yes. And now we live together. I am a bridge. My son died before his time. My first of three boys. I quit smoking some years after that, though at times I crave it like I crave rye bread, like I crave sanity and compassion in our elected officials. We eat munn cookies and laugh at the latest world war. In the Arctic, we would chip ice into our glasses right from the glacier, she says.

The Elevator Dream

I'm in a small Southern Ontario city looking at apartments. I have a cup of ice that I am chewing from. We go up the elevators, see the apartments, go down the elevators. I keep chewing the ice, which isn't depleting.

Now we are driving along country roads in the middle of the night, the news of the death fresh as the cool Georgian Bay air. We drive through tall trees, past secret lakes, under condemned bridges, puddles of darkness that the headlights cannot or will not reach pooling at every dip in the road.

Now I'm standing on the Brooklyn Bridge. I am alone. The city is blooming backwards and forwards in time. From trees to skyscrapers to trees, Wall St. to wall, Canal to canal, pre-contact to Seventies dilapidation. I'm worried the bridge itself will disappear, that the city will fragment, the rebar of subways melt away. But for now it holds. I have a decision to make: cross into the city or head for the outer boroughs, the island that eventually ends in a sharp nub of sand and rock. I wait. The sun sets.

I wait.

The Procession Dream

There's a lineup to the coffin. Each person puts in one item: the keys to her house; dried wild flowers; the yellow and red IMPEACH sign forgotten in the attic; the collected Alice Munro; the collected Pete Seeger; playbills from a lifetime of playbills; a piece of stone chiseled from the Brooklyn Bridge; a photo of her grandchildren; hair rollers; a pack of Parliaments; a bottle of Clinique Aromatics Elixir; a box of Peace Calendars; a box of Bev Doolittle calendars, birthdays and plays and doctor appointments and poetry classes written in her fine scrawl; rye bread; munn cookies; Zabar's dark roast coffee beans; coffee cake; a gallon of NYC water, the best tap water in the world; an assortment of New York cheeses; another rye bread; the desk she and Morty shared, where he spent nights studying for his PhD thesis on reforming adult education, where she marked homework, where they tried, in their own small way, to do something. Once the coffin is lowered into the earth, we each lift a shovelful of dirt.

The Question Dream

Have I ever told you how we met?
Have I ever told you how we met?

The Window Dream

I was at my desk, I think, some sort of desk, and I was typing. I typed: *Her name was Frances Kreuter. She knew the name of every wildflower. The men in her life all had bad hearts. She married Morty in the basement of a shul on Ocean Parkway. She was involved in establishing the first New York City teachers' union. She fought against racism, classism, and homophobia her entire life. When she'd cross the border and visit us in Toronto, she would always bring gifts from her travels, an American fifty-dollar bill for each of us, gleefully exchanged for Canadian dollars, sometimes doubled in value. She died still fighting.* I stop writing and look out the window. A giant bird is soaring through the sky. Seeing the bird makes me realize I was dreaming: it was much too big, much too high, for it to be anything but a dream. I think about this for a moment, decide it doesn't matter. I go back to the work.

She knew the name of every wildflower, I type.

I.

Grandfathers never met, never known.
New York and Montreal, island and island,
a two-mouthed beast whose offspring
moved to mid-town Toronto.
Dead from cancer, dead from an exploding heart.
Route lines to Ukraine, to the Pale, to Hamburg.
An educator radical communist navy man,
an owner of a small paper factory and a father of four.
The first high school on Riker's Island.
A Yiddishite revue at the winter theatre.
From the projects to Bayside, Queens.
From St. Urbain Street to Côte Saint-Luc,
a small piece of land abutting Lake Champlain,
a salmon-pink trailer, weekends over
the bridge and border to wife, daughters, son.
Grandfathers, never met, never known.

II.

Grandfathers dead from cancer.
Grandfathers dead from exploding hearts.
Grandfathers at a march for Ethel Rosenberg.
Grandfathers in blackface.
Grandfathers who fell in love with grandmothers.
Grandfathers who fell in love with other grandfathers.
Grandfathers who will never be grandfathers.
Grandfathers who walked and walked and walked.
Grandfathers who read too many think pieces.
Grandfathers who religiously follow casting calls,
to track which TV programs will eventually stage orgies.
Grandfathers who survived dehumanization in the name of purity.
Grandfathers who hate Arabs.
Grandfathers who do not acknowledge
the unceded land under their slippered feet.
Grandfathers pouring microbeads into the ocean.
Grandfathers who have drunk too much Kool-Aid.
Grandfathers who invented Kool-Aid.
Grandfathers storing grain for the coming famine.
Grandfathers doing what they're told.

III.

It's easy to blame the grandfathers (founding fathers, forefathers) without acknowledging the grandfather in each of us. Think of it as a chain. Think of it as a staircase. Grandfathers, and their grandfathers, and their grandfathers' grandfathers, all the way back to the grandfather muck— undivided, fragrant grandfather potential—to the original shallow pool dreaming the original grandfather epic (it'll have everything—sacrifice! perseverance! hierarchy! strip malls!). And there I am, and there you are, too. And we're sorry for everything, even though here we are, our fingers on the trigger, the launch codes keyed in, feeling kind of reckless.

It's well known that most shows hit their stride in the third season, but here we are midway through the first and cancellation looms. But what can we do to appease the fickle hearts of the great network execs in the sky? Despite all the plot holes, despite all the corruption, all the one-dimensional villains, all the burned and rotted set pieces, all the unimaginable bloodletting, we still have potential, do we not? The entirely human potential of good (not great) television. So for now, I guess we'll keep going, keep scripting meet-cutes and emotional confrontations by a roiling sea, stage one-offs at a volcano, the toilets of an interplanetary spacecraft, the breadline. And in our quieter moments, we'll imagine when this is all over: the studios empty, the warehouses of props, wigs, and exploding cigars gathering dust, the writers'-room tables hacked into firewood, actors performing around bonfires, producers in jail, executive producers governors of small oil-producing states, when, for the first time in its nearly eighty years, the television river will be dried up, the phrase "I'll come up at the next commercial" never to be uttered again. No more cathode ray tubes, no more collective dreams. And yet, even then, our once-beloved shows will be emanating out into the cosmos, an imperfect memory of laugh tracks and state hangings and haunting beauty, there for anybody who decides to tune in, a school of shimmering fish rising from the deep.

"Cousinage: A Meet Cute": The idea of carrying a "shtetl on your back" comes from the opening scene of *Angels in America*.

"A Day in the Life of a High Complexity Burn Boss": I encountered the pamphlet quoted in the epigraph in the foyer of my friend Tal's apartment, right across the street from High Park.

"Icelandic for Not Another Poem about Iceland":
Read the Sagas. Seriously, they're amazing.

"Acid Trip in a Porta-potty": This particular porta-potty journey most likely took place at a Phish festival.

"Capitalism Gets an Origin Story": The image of capitalism turning everything solid into thin air is from *The Communist Manifesto*.

"Get Away from Me, Television": The quote about one of the great TV genres is from the *Vulture* article "The Return of the Episodic Anthology Series" by Josef Adalian. "What is an automobile" is riffing on the famous Talking Heads song "Once in a Lifetime."

"South Florida": The mention of rainbows rainbows rainbows is an allusion to Elizabeth Bishop's "The Fish." The Seminole Wars are . . . well, you should google it.

"My Father Philosophizes. . ." is dedicated to all the wait staff at all the Cheesecake Factorys in all the world.

"Montreal": The Richler collection is *The Street*.

"To a Palestinian Cousin": Marita, and the waiting for her, is a reference to the Leonard Cohen poem, "Marita."

ACKNOWLEDGEMENTS

Some of the poems appeared, in sometimes slightly different form, in the following journals and magazines. Thank you to the editors. "Acid Trip in a Porta-potty" appeared in *The Puritan*. "Bonetown" appeared in ARC. "Capitalism Gets an Origin Story" appeared in *Humber Literary Review*. "Côte Saint-Luc Road" appeared in *Big Smoke Poetry*. "Cousinage" appeared in *Pithead Chapel*. "Discarded Novel Openings" appeared in *Echolocation*. "Dreams I Had the Week before My Grandmother Passed Away" and "Sure-fire Signs Your Loved One is a Cellphone User" appeared in *The Hart House Review*. "Eighteen Ways of Looking at Magneto Destroying Auschwitz in *X-Men: Apocalypse*" appeared in *Long Con Magazine*. "Icelandic for Not Another Poem about Iceland" appeared in *Train*. "Shifting Baseline Syndrome" appeared in *Vallum* and was reprinted in *Watch Your Head*. "The Last Six Minutes of the Nature Documentary, Where David Attenborough Tells Us the Beautiful Animals We've Just Been Watching Are Dying, and It's All Our Fault" appeared in *Bad Dog*. "The Professor of Ontology" appeared in *Poetry Is Dead*. "@Herzl1860" appeared in *Jewish Currents Poetry Anthology 2018*.

"Dreams I Had the Week before My Grandmother Passed Away" appeared in the *Not Another Cancer Anthology*, edited by Priscilla Uppal. "Hydrophobia" appeared in *Sweetwater: Poems for the Watershed*, edited by Yvonne Blomer. "Cousinage: A Meet Cute" was included in the "notable" list in *Best Canadian Poetry 2019*.

To start, I must acknowledge and thank everybody at University of Regina Press and the Oskana Poetry & Poetics imprint. My deepest thanks to Randy Lundy, my editor, who gave the book a loving home and a careful eye. Thank you as well to Kelly Laycock, Karen Clark, and Duncan Campbell. I also must thank Catriona Wright, who edited *Shifting Baseline Syndrome* in an earlier form. Your mark remains on these poems! Thanks to Andy Verboom, for designing the fish on the cover.

Thanks to my family: my parents, Cath Kreuter and David Kreuter, who have always been there for me, and are, without a doubt, my biggest fans, my greatest supporters; my siblings, Ben Kreuter, Rebecca Garber, Rachel Kreuter, Sam Berns, Jenn Korn, Jon Geiger, and the Ds (Daniel Korn and Dana Brodsetter). To Susan Korn and Mark Korn.

To Myra Bloom, Eric Schmaltz, David Huebert, Dan Sadowski, Tyler Ball, Jeff Ebedia, Kristina Getz, Tal Davidson, Rob Goodman.

To Steph, my best friend, my partner; you've known these poems from their earliest drafts, from lines yelled at and laughed at. To Piper, canine cousin extraordinaire. To my grandparents, Morty and Fran Kreuter, Phil and Edna Borden.

To Noa.

AARON KREUTER is the author of the short story collection *You and Me, Belonging* (2018) and the poetry collection *Arguments for Lawn Chairs* (2016). His writing has appeared in places such as *Grain Magazine, The Puritan, The Temz Review,* and *The Rusty Toque.* Kreuter lives in Toronto, where he is assistant fiction editor at *Pithead Chapel,* and a postdoctoral fellow at Carleton University. *Shifting Baseline Syndrome* is his second book of poems.

ᐅᓇᐸ

OSKANA POETRY & POETICS
BOOK SERIES

Publishing new and established authors, Oskana Poetry
& Poetics offers both contemporary poetry at its best
and probing discussions of poetry's cultural role.

Randy Lundy—*Series Editor*

Advisory Board

Sherwin Bitsui   Tim Lilburn
Robert Bringhurst   Duane Niatum
Laurie D. Graham   Gary Snyder
Louise Bernice Halfe   Karen Solie

PREVIOUS BOOKS IN THE SERIES:

Measures of Astonishment: Poets on Poetry,
presented by the League of Canadian Poets (2016)

The Long Walk, by Jan Zwicky (2016)

Cloud Physics, by Karen Enns (2017)

The House of Charlemagne, by Tim Lilburn (2018)

Blackbird Song, by Randy Lundy (2018)

Forty-One Pages: On Poetry, Language and Wilderness,
by John Steffler (2019)

Live Ones, by Sadie McCarney (2019)

Field Notes for the Self, by Randy Lundy (2020)

Burden, by Douglas Burnet Smith (2020)

Red Obsidian, by Stephan Torre (2021)

Pitchblende, by Elise Marcella Godfrey (2021)

Shifting Baseline Syndrome, by Aaron Kreuter (2022)

Synaptic, by Alison Calder (2022)